www.finishinglinepress.com

Things Haven't Been the Same

Poems

by

Ralph Stevens

Finishing Line Press
Georgetown, Kentucky

Things Haven't Been the Same

Poems

Publisher: Leah Maines

Editor: Christen Kincaid

Cover Photo: Clint McKoy on Unsplash

Author Photo: Sally Rowan

Cover Design: Rebecca Powell

Printed in the USA on acid-free paper.
Order online: www.finishinglinepress.com
            also available on amazon.com

Author inquiries and mail orders:
Finishing Line Press
P. O. Box 1626
Georgetown, Kentucky 40324
U. S. A.

Table of Contents

for Sally

The Whippoorwill

A little boy, I
once lay in the dark
in the echoing time
after the grown-ups
had gone to bed.
A whippoorwill,
calling from the woods
seemed to know this,
that I was still awake,
and had only him
for company.

Prophecy

Of places desolate and void
their minds were full,
those prophets, place
of the owl, land
of whirring wings.
Or so I think, reading late,
the wine still sitting there,
untouched. The old dog paces,
claws clicking unsteadily.
My daughter watches him circle,
making his bed, while prophecy
arrives uninvited,
dressed in rags,
asking for my voice.

Notes from the Underground

Robin stalks the graveyard next door,
indifferent to death as is
the life he hears, head cocked,
small bodies
rising to the April breeze.

Something I barely hear
is always chirping, always
scuttling with fierce purpose
across my cellar floor, circling,
finding invisible morsels.

Rules of the Game

Keep your eyes open and don't
describe what isn't there.

A rose is still a rose.
Let the creek flow as it likes,

and like nothing else—
and words are always

one remove from the flavor of figs
still warm in the sun.

Let's go back
to the primal sounds

of pain and wonder—
"Ahh!" and "Ooh!" the sound

of snow falling where
there's no one to hear it.

Making Sense of Things

That spider, for instance—she's
been hanging in the window
for a week now without moving.
Those rows of sand dollars
on the picnic table: there's no one
in the house now but
there they are,
morning after morning
when I walk that way.
And the giant spruce
lying helpless on the forest floor,
its web of roots
rising above my head.
Not a blow-down from the storm
that came and went this week—it's
been there for years and still
no sign of rot and, after all,
perhaps I don't need
to make sense of things.
The mind could find rest
in this garden of mere fact,
the motionless spider,
bleaching sand dollars,
the waiting tree.

Bedtime

Much of what we call living
we learned at bedtime.
At first we didn't want to go,
held fast by toys on the rug.
It was temptation
broke us free, Mommy
promising a story
but first we had to brush our teeth,
learning that everything has a price.
The trade-off was the reading,
the body beside us on the couch,
and the piggyback ride
making us forget
the solitary bed upstairs.
The tucking-in, the goodnight kiss,
were pleasant distractions but
nothing would keep the light
from going out,
or keep imagination
from populating the dark.

Fresh Asphalt

When we kids got mixed up with
some fresh asphalt and
might have been Brer Rabbit
stuck in the Tar Baby, Stan,
the grown up, found us.
He thought it punishment enough
to scrub our blackened hands and
knees with turpentine. This was
before school and in another life,
but the smell of turpentine still holds
those August afternoons, pavement
as hot on our bare feet as the stream
running beneath the bridge
was cool.

Secret Sharer

The day will come when
you get home,
tired from work, feeling
disconnected and your daughter,
three years old and perhaps
knee high, will run up
and grab your leg.
She hangs on so tight you
think she's afraid you
might pull away
into the no-daughter-land
of TV and whisky but instead she
holds out her hand and looks up.
She only wants to see if
you see the shell,
shades of purple on the outside
like a dark sunset, the inside
white as the spray of the big
waves they watched in silence,
she and her mother,
at the beach that morning.

Staying Upright

How can you
anticipate a fall?
Gravel could be
spilling from a driveway
as you lean into the turn.
You never know.
And in farm country
a crawling tractor,
dragging a harrow
just over that blind rise. Things
come to a sudden halt.
Just past Manor Tavern the road is
lovely, sun shining, pavement dry.
But in your head something's
not right. There could be
wet leaves in the shadows of those
maples as you
eye the fine line
between what you see and
the darkness in your mind,
where you keep your balance.

Flotsam and Jetsam

Say you're walking on the beach and find
a Pepsi can or
a flip flop with a broken strap,
a bait bag washed ashore
from a lobsterman's traps.
Hang these on the decapitated spruce
beside the boardwalk
where it crosses the marsh,
and comes to an old door in the woods.
You now have
honored the flotsam and jetsam
of your life; you are ready
for what lies beyond
that door.

In the Darkness of a Distant Farm

The stories begin
where things are lost.
That rifle you hunted with as a boy—
don't go looking for it or
you'll be back in the woods again,
and it won't be the same woods
anymore. What's left is
the story of that boy.

Doesn't something always
keep you from resting, some loss
that makes you want to pick up a guitar,
walk to the beach where children
hunch over tide pools, something
with a story in it?

Take this ancient car,
black, with red wheels, dust
still coating the fenders from
some forgotten race.
It was sold years ago,
but an old man remembers
how it sat on the rough,
wide boards of the barn floor
in the darkness of a distant farm,
smelling of hot oil.

Perhaps even now he's
making up a story.

Gravity

I doubt he feels it, not
if I correctly read
that head-high trot,
easy lope beside me—
or is he beside himself,
with delight at smells he
never knew existed,
just as he knows nothing of his weight,
the fur-covered seventy pounds
of flesh and bone, or
for that matter, my weight that
lumbers toward the ocean,
the shattering water,
writing into every step
the history of love gone sour,
failure at the bank, of
staying in the game
when the deck has gone cold.

Beside the Frozen Brook

Why am I hungry for something,
blank sky, black ice of this frozen brook?
In January I am empty as a deer's skull
dropped when the wolves moved on.
Feed me, I say to the moss that forms
the forest floor, its soft greens
unseasonably warm, its silence
forcing the words back.
And why should I be reassured
by two crows that shoot ahead of me,
strafing the trail
with the shadow of their wings?

Consent Form

The consent form is casting
shadows over the field trip.
Sixth graders stand in kitchens
across town, entrusting parents
with the bright promise of a day
like no other, and there it is,
captured in black and white
on paper now handed up,
the words "explore," "learn,"
"to the lake," "at the museum, the beach
the fairgrounds," "pack a sweater,
a snack," words of release
from lives at plastic desks
in rooms where, day after day,
the maps hanging on the walls
never change. These eager children
will not read the fine print, the last
words above the blank
where Mom or Dad will sign,
words on the underside
of this bright rock:
"some risk of trauma," "possible
dismemberment," "accidental death,"
and will said parent agree to
"indemnify," "not hold responsible now
or at any future time…"?
Pens in hand, parents
fold their children's lives
into these slips of paper,
tuck them into backpacks
with the sandwiches and sweaters,
above their legal, dated, names.

The Marsh in a Thunderstorm

What sort of courage does it take
to brave the marsh in a thunderstorm?
What makes it worse in pelting rain,
lightning striking from all sides,
than parking lots at malls,
playgrounds with your children?
On city streets a quick dash
to the nearest doorway,
a frantic fumble for the car keys,
and you're safe.
But in the marsh,
wide open under a sky
growing darker by the second,
the path lost in tangled grass, afternoon
disappearing in gusts of wind,
you are no ordinary pedestrian
caught in a summer shower.

Crime Tape

It's not as if I
don't know
how things turn out.
The crime tape goes up,
the divider, crowd
on one side, child's
body on the other,
lying in the rain, detective
standing over her
stone-faced.
It's not as if I don't know
the dirty pavement,
sullen sky,
sense of justice
broken again.
This is how things are—
among discarded needles, crack vials.
The child's killer
won't be found.
The wounded heart
stays wounded.
We all are lost
when one is lost,
and that's the way it is,
how things turn out, here,
at the crime tape.

The Lost Are like This

In here the walls
are not white or
stained with blood.
The ceiling has no
staring light.
You feel the April
sun through the bars,
hear the birds
waking up to build their nests,
but the tightness in your chest
reads like a suicide note.
The man with the questions
wears no black gloves, carries
no truncheon, but his smile
is like road kill.
In your head is what
butterflies know,
struggling damply to escape their cocoons,
but you are speechless as he
asks you who you
think you are,
just what it is
you might become.

In the Dislodging Wind

Living and dying are the same
if it's true we all belong
somewhere
in the end.
But what if
sitting here drinking a cup of coffee
grown cold as I write, I look up
to see the room has vanished, the walls,
windows gone, the shelves,
cabinets, all the places things are kept,
gone, and there is no more
belonging? What if
living and dying disappear and I
am left alone in the dislodging wind
now rising in the east?

It's All Now for the Crow

The time came when I was ready
to negotiate with terror.
I was standing in the kitchen peeling carrots,
shavings dropping into the sink. I was
watching a crow through the window
strutting across the lawn
fearless, yet if I
reached for the rifle
standing in the corner
he'd be in a tree before my hand
closed around the grip. He knew—
in the way of crows—
about the gun just as he knew
about me, picking up a knife
to slice the carrots
for the boeuf bourguignon.
His dark eye takes the moment
with all its dangers, seeing each
raised stick, stalking foot.
But it's all here and now
for the crow, I thought
as I shook half a bottle of Bordeaux
into the stew.
What the crow doesn't see is
the time to come, the time when
a dam upstream will burst,
skyscrapers fall in a torrent of fire,
and we wash out, we burn,
crow and I.
So I was ready,
as I took the kettle
bubbling from the oven,
for the knock on the door.
"May I come in?"
said Terror.
"It's time we talked."

Catching the Lip of Snow

It was winter and I was on my own
in a wide field, stubble
showing through the snow.
It was before breakfast, and I
was walking with no direction home,
but the brown stalks
were something to focus on.
Nothing moved, there was no
sound beyond a boot breaking crust,
toe catching the lip of snow as each foot
came free. This was how I walked,
dropping into each lurching step,
finding a kind of direction.

Solving for the Unknown

lying sleepless in the dark
a cage of sound
around the bed

the equation
writes itself
in variables
flutter in the eaves
refrigerator
going off distant
barking perhaps
hum of passing car and

insomniac mathematician I
write an algebra of sound
solving for the unknown

Visiting the Lighthouse

At times we thought it best
to enumerate old themes—
beauty at the wheel of the Cadillac,
red hair flying, crows
restless in the tops of spruce,
conducting the family business.
Nothing was settled
but we were only tourists,
climbing the iron stairs
to the lantern room,
inspecting the first order
Fresnel lens. We saw
the rented chairs
set up for a wedding, saw
the bride on the rocks below us,
looking past the camera
at the sea.

Pruning

I told myself there must be
classrooms where the dead
instruct the living, perhaps
offering a lesson on
the apple tree my dad
kept pruning until he
knew he was alive,
and I might live like that,
gathering dead branches
from all the trees out there where
the fathers sail with the moon where
people pick apples
in the darkness
of another life.

After a Day of Rain

traffic huddles home,
muffled by a season without echoes.
At the bridge,
a woman crossing from town,
someone you knew in high school,
her face now scarved from sight,
blurred by the wipers.
In French she
smelled of wet wool, her hair
reckless on the desk
in front of you.
"J'entre dans la salle de classe—"
Her voice could be
footsteps in an orchard—but
"Tu ne les entends plus."

Someone has left the porch light on.
In the aftermath of rain,
the engine off, window down,
there is only the ritard of water
dripping from the eaves—music
reviving in the darkness
where all notes hang,
ready to fall.

Pond Ice

It's a mystery
how a song begins
lodging in the ear while you are
peeling apples for a pie,
running the vacuum cleaner,
or walking in the woods.
There's a moment when you
ignore the apples,
the dust under the sofa,
when the trees move quietly aside,
the house, whatever state it's in,
clean or disorderly, and you
relax the way dad
relaxed at his workbench,
humming while he
shaped a piece of pine
into a small
shelf for a clock.
So you turn the peeler,
spin the fruit
into rings of white apple flesh,
and something in your chest
gives way to song,
like pond ice sinking in April
when it lets go of the shore.

The Water Is Wide

"But that was in another country."
He yawned. "Or at least another city,
and besides, the girl is dead."

Or was it simply
another state of mind,
and of course she's not really dead,
not literally,
and every now and then
the mind goes back
to the day they rented a skiff with
two seats so both could row,
and made their way to the middle of the lake,
to a small island.
There was a wooden dock, old, but
the planks were warm and still intact.
They made fast and climbed up,
stood there for a while
looking back across the water
barely touching. Yet that
was enough, standing together
in that wideness.
Does it matter that it was
a long time ago?

Rumi's Field

Out beyond ideas of right doing and wrong doing,
there is a field. I will meet you there.
       Rumi

I was standing in the field where Rumi
said he would meet me.
It was late and snowing hard
so I thought the poet might have cancelled
or decided to obey the turnpike warnings
to slow to forty-five and not
crowd the plows.
The flakes were big ones,
dropping slowly, covering
the spruce and fir that fenced us,
me and the field, and I thought about
a picture I saw once of markings
in fresh snow where an owl
had dropped on a field mouse,
leaving the image of
claws and spread wings.
I began to wonder if
I was in the right field but
he might be here already,
the poet,
just waiting for the
right moment
to drop on me.

Magnetic Resonant Image

This lying here, trapped,
plastic cocoon around my
head jammed between sponge pads
stirs me to action mind
fighting stasis gasp—
ing for intellectual breath
a drowning swimmer
struggling for the surface,
flailing against the knocking hammering
machine gun stuttering
through the ear plugs.
So the plug comes out of
song, poetry, lines from Milton
Shakespeare running breathlessly
with Donne, with Keats, Hardy
Dickinson, Frost to tell the
shadow images now forming
in digital non-space that
body lives and moves
and has its being anywhere the
mind can move, can
form a thought, hear
perfect triads, rhyming
couplets, see a resonant
image of
something that flies from
any burst cocoon.

Herald Angel

Snow falling in sunlight
startles this January morning into action.
I climb into the cellar
flooded in a recent storm and begin
digging out the victims like people
trapped in the rubble of an earthquake,
soggy boxes of family papers we
never stored when we moved—
old bank statements,
notebooks from graduate school
forty years old and barely legible.
Hard to move in one piece,
the boxes sag, flood-heavy. Thank
God these are only paper and not
flesh and blood casualties,
I think, remembering real floods
that breach levees along swollen rivers,
take out houses, sweep entire
parishes. All I mourn are some bleared
notes on Wordsworth, drafts of old
poems, a sheaf of letters
from my father, while the snow
drifts slowly down against a blue sky,
like feathers of a herald angel
who might show up
any moment now.

The Oak Chest

After a day spent wandering
the fields of my house,
exploring the often-explored, knowing
there was something I'd not yet
discovered, I stop in front of the
oak chest that was my father's.
It was green when I was a boy,
a landmark on trips through the shop
to the barn. For him
it was a place to store
cans of paint, neatly stacked,
scrapers, sandpapers and paint brushes,
tools for creating color.
The chest now has no color, or,
I should say, no paint.
He scraped off the green
sometime after I went to college,
seeing beneath the bright enamel
the antique commode it once was,
house of thick towels, ladies' soap and hair
brushes where he now kept turpentine,
varnish and lacquer.
He was slow and patient, my father,
a man for whom time disappeared in precise
strokes of the scraper blade and the timeless
grain of oak. Staring now into those
open pores I see why
he never finished the job, why he
stopped once the wood was free of paint,
declined the customary colors
that might turn the light away.

The Eye of the Crow

New evidence about nature
turns up unexpectedly.
I thought that crows
preferred the upper branches
of the lofty trees—the elm, maple,
the pointed spruce. After all
wariness requires the wider view.
But today a crow
lands low in an apple tree.
An eagle circles high above,
so this perch might be a sign
of deference to talons
and a greater wing span.
Or perhaps he just
likes the shriveled apples
that hang there
catching his eye.

The Forces of Nature

sleep in the shadows
of these trees, in
moss pillows that line black
hollows where the water
has no place to go, sits still
and unreflecting. Perhaps nature
will wake up in rotting
bodies of trees downed long ago.
Today the wind is an abstraction,
a sighing, distant and aloof, broken
into barely audible breaths.
There will be a time
when air gathers resolution,
grabs the tops of trees,
and shakes the sleep out of the nerveless earth.
I sit on a stump at ground zero,
studying the tall
gray poles of spruce,
picturing the wind
seizing the giant lever of each trunk,
ripping the forest floor
from its roots.

A Murder of Crows

It would be easy to miss, that dark
shadow in the stand of spruce but
a murder of crows keeps attacking,
each one diving, strafing the trees,
stalling, climbing, diving again,
their angry cries drawing the eye.
And the eye resolves the shadow—
an eagle five times crow size,
unmoving in the branches,
from where I stand the mere outline
of a crow's bad dream.

Long Winter

A loon sits motionless in a cold sea
that can't sit still, rolling and lunging
with an energy even granite rocks
must feel. The long beak turns now and then
an unblinking eye staring
at what I can only imagine. So I do,
having tried it on the white
birches along the road,
bent by a recent storm,
studying earth from a different perspective.
The loon needs no imagination
to know wind and water,
schools of herring, the coming spring,
his mate, the inland lakes where
they will nest, leaving me, my
blood talking back to the long winter,
months of snow without promise—blood
falling into its own vascular wilderness.

Taking Flight: Two Birds

After photographs by Eliot Porter

The Sparrow

is in flight,
gray wings fanned against
green leaves, its eye
alert, beak
pointed in purpose.
Legs and claws—
things sharp and clutching—
disappear beneath the wing fan,
its broad palms open,
hands without fingers,
spread like the stumps of vanished thumbs.
What else has he lost,
with wings that once
sprouted tiny arm and talon,
hand-me-downs
from reptilian forebears?
He depends on nothing
more solid than the landings of air
as he flies off, leaving tiny hatchlings,
blind, colorless, their huge mouths stretched
wider than their heads.

The Osprey

hovers over one chick, wings
stretched like a victory banner,
tail feathers ruling the sky.
Across the eyes a black bar
balances the claws below,
opened in rapture. It astonishes,
this power over air and I
pin my hopes on that chick,
looking up at the father,
certain of its next meal.

Imagining Orca

None of those whales cavorting in
Puget Sound will ever win
the Peace Prize,
but see how joyfully
they greet that clump of skiffs
angling off Point No Point in the rain.
Here must be fish, they say,
feeling their voices loosen up,
feeling the Arctic pour
unratified off their flukes.
They dive and soar,
schooling the green dark,
and singing, as the fleet trembles,
as fishermen gape at great
statesmen of the Orca tribe
negotiating with tiny boats of
fiberglass and pine, singing
welcome,
welcome to our kingdom!

Argos

The spring robins have begun
their work on the lawn,
eating the grubs that eat the roots of my
tender grass. Soon the deer
will arrive, the ones who
eye the lettuce taking root in our gardens
as they do every spring,
as they did for Homer's Greeks
in the cycle of life our gardens
share with theirs.
Spring is always spring no
matter how the world changes,
and those ancients had their robins, their
insect infestations, had words
for their disgust with whatever
eats the joy of light lengthening,
grass appearing. They knew with us
the grubs but also knew
the thrush and owl,
heard their mating calls
in the spring night.
"And they had the same old dog," I think,
"the one who lifts his head when I come in
as Argos on the dung heap did
when Odysseus
finally made it home."

Walking the Dog

I like to think I'm working but
I'm just waiting for the dog
to say he wants to go outside.
The house is chilly, this October
morning, so I'll light a fire first.
The dog being young and heedless will
race back and forth across the trail
into pools that fill the hollows
after recent rain, floundering where
the water's deeper than he expected.
I'll stick to the path, skirt these
water holes, and contemplate my envy
for this animal whose nose
makes him alive to a different world,
working through each forest scent
with no concern for work. Yet in the end
we will be one, dog and I,
back at my desk,
he resting by my feet
in the now warm house.

Waiting for the Wind to Drop

Today the dog held his barking
while I got dressed.
We went out in the rain,
along a path covered with moss,
a surprising green beneath the dark
arms of spruce. Our way
ended on the rocks
high above the sea where
the rain ran nearly flat
across the waves.
It was good, with the dog
patient beside me,
to see the whole of it,
wind and rain spread out
in the grey-green of sky,
with no fear of the night to come,
when I would lie awake,
waiting for the wind to drop,
listening for whatever night bird
might be calling.

St. Ambrose Church, Tichborne, March 24, AD 2003

At Stonehenge the sun's rays
no longer strike the altar
at the solstice. So the stars
don't always stay their courses?
An English breakfast
of fried tomatoes, eggs and
black pudding will remain in place
long enough to get us through the morning.
At St. Ambrose Church where
Sir Benjamin lies entombed,
it's March 24th, four centuries to the day
since the death of Queen Elizabeth,
this knight's earthly lord except
she was a lady. Names change
as well as stars, and things
are not always what we call them,
however we search for constancy.
At St. Ambrose where the dead
hang on by virtue of polished stone,
prayers offered centuries ago
expand by virtue of a force
that never changes,
while over Stonehenge
the shifting moon may yet,
for all we know,
be where the dead stop a while
when they've grown restless
in their marble vaults.

Into Falling Snow

In one scene, the diners
go into falling snow,
and dance around the well.
A small boy
is afraid to climb into a small boat,
in a notch of quiet water.
Particles of mercy
cover a city of fire
at laundry time,
in the washing and folding of clothes.
I am twice-born, in an allegory of wings,
responsible for interpretation,
disturbed by the sense of hands
on which fingers have become feathers.
A stone falls into the well,
speaks volumes in the hour
after sunrise, when crows and gulls
start arguing.
We reach out to battlefields,
asylums, slums,
allegorists of pain.
"Daddy, what are the words after
'Off they hurry, flying'?"
She is nesting with the once-born,
reaching her tiny hand for quarters
to get the washing started.

The Phases of the Moon

With how sad steps, O Moon, thou climb'st the skies,
How wearily, and with how wan a face...
Philip Sidney

But it is only we who are sad,
who suffer change like the warbler
that broke its neck just now
against the picture window
in the changing light of evening.
She went quickly from song to silence.
The moon has always been the moon,
always full, dark on one side, light on the other.
It's our view that changes, and
perhaps his smile is not for us at all.
He has the larger view, that man in the moon,
his eye on bigger things, unchanging while
we live with these appearances,
leaves turning red and falling, neighbors
loading the moving van, the ice cap
melting, and notice all that
renovation going on, art deco theaters
restored to glory, garment factories
becoming condos, and what's sad
isn't change but how we crave it,
moving to stay alive, changing
into clean clothes every morning,
getting with what's
trending on the Internet,
marking the changes,
like phases
of the moon.

Kingdom

We drove for hours in the rain.
When the sun came out we found
a stretch of median like a pasture
sloping toward the eastbound lanes,
the grass recovering from a recent mowing.
We defied the odds, pulled off,
knowing whatever city
we were bound for could wait.
In a clump of scrub pine
we ate our bread, drank a little wine
while traffic flowed around us
like an ocean breathing, surf on another shore,
where the pieces of a broken marriage
are picked up, and no one cries
in the room where someone's legs
grow yellow in the last stage of cancer,
no one stares at the rug,
in the arctic whiteness of despair.
We bagged our litter,
leaned against the fender for a while
then started the engine,
kingdom-bound.

The Long Habit of Living

is hard to break, although
some life we could do without,
like that white SUV blocking my driveway—
and what's up with the sitcom?
Even the good ones get old.
Seinfeld went off the air, finally,
and for some of us
old doesn't take long,
a few episodes maybe, but
what about the harbor seals
sunning on the rocks,
the overture to *Don Giovanni*
or a walk-off home run?
In the long run we're
indisposed when death arrives.
Perhaps we're expected to equate
the good with the bad and the ugly.
After all, twelve bars of B.B. King, one
perfect wave off Waikiki
can solve the equation.
If thinking makes it so, then why not
make it all good with one fair thought,
even the thought of death,
rising like an invisible sun
within us.

Fresh Figs

In memory of Malcolm Donald

My neighbor is going into town
to buy fresh figs. Not plentiful,
fresh figs, in this latitude where
in August the sun ripens a little corn, tomatoes,
and warms the barrens long enough
to color the wild blueberries
our bit of continent is famous for.
He wheels an oxygen tank,
my neighbor,
stops to catch a breath
before climbing from the dock.
He talks between gasps of his days
in Algeria, Turkey, Tunisia, where
fresh figs are thick as the herring
in our northern waters, and
there was a time the local grocers
knew all the trade routes
to golden orchards of the Mediterranean.
But the fig-loving population
has died off, he says, that
used to keep demand pumped up.
Now he waits on market forces
indifferent to the tongue's subtle longings,
as are the gouts of oxygen
filing into the remaining spaces
in his lungs.

North Carolina Road

It's hard to write about the dead and perhaps you will
forgive me if I make it brief. His life
was brief. There isn't much to tell,
only that he loved motorcycles, their heat and smell,
the rush of North Carolina air against his face
as he rode at night. There were other roads we cut,
he and I, for toy trucks in the dirt behind the house
when we were boys, before he was run down in the dark
by a man he never knew. He was courteous, loyal to his friends
as in Da Nang when they'd get stoned in the rockets' red glare.
Going home he had a Hong Kong tailor dress his Marine blues
with delicate gold and red and green flowers—a gesture
not to the flower children of that era, but to a soldier's kinship
with what cannot be killed.

She Establishes Herself

although uncertain of the fact that this is home.
"I'm quite comfortable here" she says, meaning
with a bowl of ice cream after dinner. We know that she
is like a child at bedtime who listens quietly
to *Good Work, Amelia Bedelia*, then keeps her head tucked
into her father's shoulder and won't look up, yet calls
a faint goodnight. She looks around, a bit dazed, then
sees something familiar. "That rug looks like mine"
she says, "but what's it doing here?"
and then wants to know who we are.
She has a keen nose for interlopers.
"We live here too" we say,
trying to get her to the rocker, to
forget her former life, in a time now out of mind.
"Would you like to sit?" we ask, leading her across the room.
Her feet shuffle, inches at a time, before she's ready,
and then sitting isn't sitting but a half-fall.
"Ooof!" she mutters, and drops.
It's late and we're getting nervous, but she just rocks,
and doesn't see us glance at the clock. "Can I keep it?"
she asks, and for a moment we're the ones confused.
"Oh, the rocker?" She smiles back. "Yes. Can I keep it?"
But of course, we say, relieved to know
she's more established than we thought
this late at night.

The King's Truck

In the room of the old woman
whose mind has taken paths
too tangled to follow,
Rosie the cat
disappears.
"Rosie, where are you?"
she asks, then
"Can you hear the truck?"
Whose truck we wonder,
hearing nothing but
Rosie's loud purr, the sighing
of spruce boughs in the falling snow.
"It's the king," she says, "he
has come to take me home."
We want to ask where home is,
knowing we cannot know,
but Rosie, who has
no trouble on strange paths,
whose ears catch the sound
of life beneath the snow, reappears,
leaping into her lap,
determined not to miss the ride
that she and the old woman
hear idling outside.

An Old Man Descends the Stairs

one step at a time his
hands clutching the rail,
eyes on that narrow stream he knows
one day he'll cross, imagined
somewhere past this stumbling.
He concentrates on the shine
of low dawn light on sideboard crystal,
anything to slow encroaching time,
stay the sun at
the right angle of reflection,
glinting as he bears down
uncertain whether dread
or longing is the right
attitude for this moment.

In Spite of Appearances

it was all very simple.
There had been the phone call,
the drive across Pennsylvania hills
in the dark, the family conference
over breakfast. His condition was
stable; we could visit, and we did,
fighting the sterile mechanism
of the critical care unit,
challenging the authority
of tubes and monitors
to reach his side.
And then it was clear—
beneath the hospital gown—
the simplicity of dying. He briefly
recognized his children,
their hands around his shoulders,
before he reached his own hand free,
palm upward in submission,
open to the light.

Beside the Lamp

The remains of the day
vanish like spilled water.
Jangling anger and
the dull ache of problems unsolved
dissolve in the distant smell
of onions frying.
A car pulls away, children
wander silently indoors.
In the meadow a foal has
stopped its prancing and
stands nose to nose
with its mother.
Clamor of voices
fades and dinner's deep well of flavor
drains away.
Beside the lamp two coins
grow large enough
to fill the treasury of sleep.

Some Day

you might wonder why
I never told you this
so I'll tell you now.
One Christmas I took the family
to a small island,
to a harbor like a coat sleeve,
long and dark, where we tied up.
The night was cold and black.
There was an owl calling,
an answering call, and the cracking
of the dock's cold timbers,
planks whiskered with frost.
The water was an inverted sky,
galaxies of phosphor stars
that reeled around the dock's
tarred, crusted legs.
There were presents
in the cabin, a small
Christmas tree but these
were hardly necessary
in the heart of such a kingdom.

Things Haven't Been the Same

not since the dog ran off and you
threw your back out
looking for him in the woods.
You were the follower, he
the dog running a crooked line
visible only to his nose, but
that's the way it is,
the man-and-dog thing.
The crooked runs with the straight,
the rough places always rough
like cobbles on a beach,
and the valleys have no thought
of exaltation, but are deep and misted
late into morning. Maybe that
is where he is, your lost dog,
on the beach, or lapping water
in some valley brook. Maybe
he's just lying in the shade
of a big chestnut, waiting,
and your back has healed,
and things really aren't the same
any more.

Notes

"Prophecy" (Page 2) The images in the opening lines allude primarily to Isaiah, chapters 14 and 18, and to the Book of Lamentations via the refrain in William Byrd's anthem, "Bow thine ear, O Lord": "Sion is wasted and brought low / Jerusalem desolate and void."

"Staying Upright" (Page 9) Manor Tavern is in Monkton, in Baltimore County Maryland. The motorcycle rider would do well not to be distracted by the beauty of the surrounding countryside.

"Flotsam and Jetsam" (Page 10) There actually is a door in the woods, a few hundred yards from the beach on Little Cranberry Island, Maine. It hangs between two trees and opens into and out of nothing except rooms in the imagination of the one who enters.

"Gravity" (Page 12) For "staying in the game / when the deck has gone cold" see Bob Dylan's "Huck's Tune."

"Crime Tape" (Page 16) was inspired by "Sandtown" by Cameron Blake, a song on his album *Fear Not*. The images of the child's body lying in the rain and the detective standing over her are from the pilot episode of the TV series *Homicide*.

"In the Dislodging Wind" (Page 18) Compare the concept of belonging in Romans 14.8, "Whether we live or die we belong to the Lord" (NIV).

"It's All Now for the Crow" (Page 19) was prompted by the refrain to "Welcome to Your Wedding Day" by Airborne Toxic Event: "We do not negotiate with terror."

"Pond Ice" (Page 25) For the image of ice sinking I am indebted to Jane Kenyon's "Ice Out" from *Let Evening Come*.

"The Water Is Wide" (Page 26) The poem is the odd result of the lines from *The Jew of Malta*, "but that was in another country; / And besides the wench is dead," running up against the well-known ballad identified in the title.

"Imaging Orca" (Page 36) There actually is a Point No Point, on the Kitsap

Peninsula overlooking Puget Sound, Washington State.

"Argos" (Page 37) See the *Odyssey*, Book 17. But I just wanted to get the dog into a poem.

"St. Ambrose Church, Tichborne" (Page 40) The conclusion refers to the ancient belief that the moon is the resting place of the souls of the dead.

"Into Falling Snow" (Page 41) The opening image of dancers around a well is from the concluding scene of Gabriel Axel's *Babette's Feast* (1988). The words "off they hurry flying" are from a lullaby, "Father Bird and Mother Bird," that I've known for longer than I can remember but whose origin I cannot find.

"The Long Habit of Living" (Page 44) The title is taken from Sir Thomas Browne's *Hydriotaphia*, Chapter V, "The long habit of living indisposeth us to dying." The concluding line is an adaptation of "Life is a pure flame, and we live by an invisible sun within us," from the same source.

"The King's Truck" (Page 48) The king's truck, heard as only a person with Alzheimer's can hear, is from an incident related by Belden Lane in *The Solitude of Fierce Landscapes* in which the author's mother describes hearing "the king's truck."

"In Spite of Appearances" (Page 50) Again, I am indebted to Jane Kenyon, to "Reading Aloud to My Father," from *Otherwise*: "…and why the dying so often reach / for something only they can apprehend."

"Things Haven't Been the Same" (Page 53) See Isaiah 40.4, the lines made familiar by Handel's *Messiah*: "every valley shall be exalted…and the crooked shall be made straight, and the rough places plain." The reader will understand that my adjustment of the prophet's meaning is intentional.

Acknowledgements and Thanks

The following poems first appeared in *Verse Virtual, An Online Community Journal of Poetry*: "Things Haven't Been the Same," "Fresh Figs," "Walking the Dog," "Some Day" (as "What I Never Told You"), "Kingdom," "Prophecy," "Rumi's Field," "Magnetic Resonant Image," and "The King's Truck."

An earlier version of "Some Day" was published in *The Maryland Review* as "Christmas Eve, San Juan Islands."

"Magnetic Resonant Image" was read on "Poems from Here," a Maine Public Radio program, by Maine's poet laureate, Wesley McNair, November 2019.

"Pond Ice," "Secret Sharer," and "Staying Upright" appeared in *The Island Reader.*

Deep gratitude to Verse-Virtual editor Firestone Fineberg for creating and encouraging the V-V "village" of poets.

Deep gratitude also to my readers, Andy Kohn, Elizabeth Phelps, Tom Bertrand, Cameron Blake, Rick Benjamin, Gonzo Beck and Gary Rainford, whose comments have helped me make this a better book.

And to Rick Benjamin, poet, teacher, friend, and encourager extraordinaire, the thanks that words cannot express, for first talking me into writing a book.

There are few satisfactions for a poet greater than that of having a reader understand the heart of his poetry. To have that reader represent it visually doubles the satisfaction. Such a reader-artist is my cover designer, Becca Powell. I am honored to have my work alongside hers.

Ralph Stevens, known locally as "Skip," lives on a Maine coastal island, a small one, in a town of about 60 year-round residents. "Year-round" because there's another group, the "summer people" of folks who come to the coast when school lets out, tripling or quadrupling the size of Islesford, as the island village is known. It's hard to determine the effect of this seasonal dynamic on poetry and the creative arts but Little Cranberry Island, like the better-known Monhegan, and as with the Maine coast generally, is a place where the arts thrive. The art of painting primarily, and primarily in the *plein aire* of summer, but also a little poetry. Stevens has done most of his work as a poet in response to this environment of granite, spruce forest and the Atlantic Ocean. And in response to a community that seems to whisper "let's make something" be it a painting, a play, a song, beautiful pottery. Or a poem.

Stevens arrived on Little Cranberry from Baltimore where he was on the faculty of Coppin State University as an English professor. The surge in online education allowed him to move while holding his faculty position and continuing to teach. Now retired, he devotes more time to looking for poems. He has been nominated for a Pushcart Prize and is the author of the collection At Bunker Cove. His poems have appeared in *The Seattle Times, Crab Creek Review, The Lyric, The Maryland Review, The Christian Century, Verse-Virtual, The Island Reader*, and on the radio programs, *The Writer's Almanac* and *Poems from Here*. Stevens is still developing an online presence and can currently be found on Facebook, and YouTube as **Ralph Skip Stevens,** https://www.youtube.com/channel/UCT8ighMHY9S27GOm9qOTenw

He can be reached by email at thismansart@gmail.com and by phone at 207.479.5843.

www.ingramcontent.com/pod-product-compliance
Lightning Source LLC
Chambersburg PA
CBHW021203090426
42740CB00008B/1211